NATURAL DISASTERS

Tsunamis

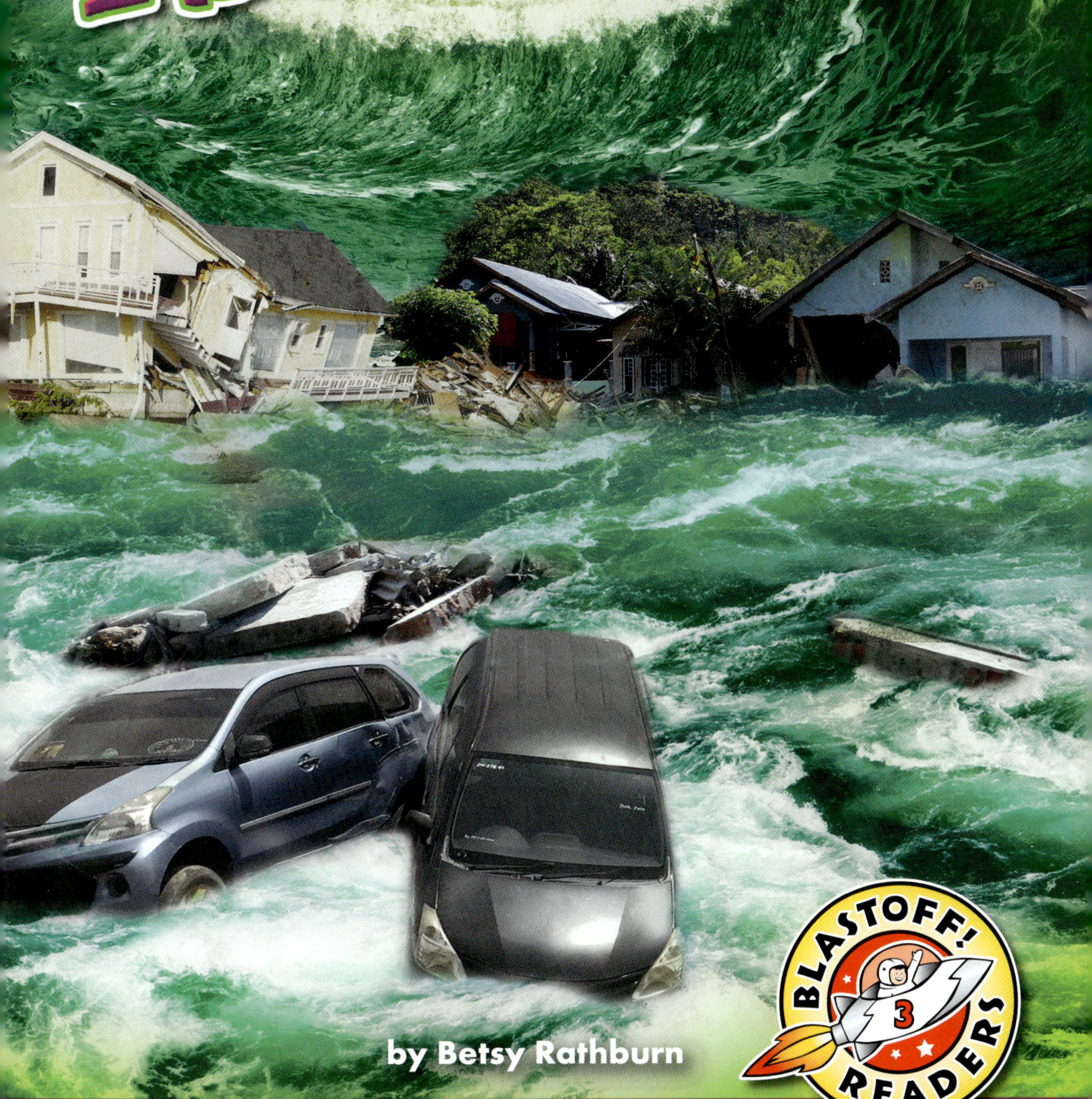

by Betsy Rathburn

BLASTOFF! READERS 3

BELLWETHER MEDIA • MINNEAPOLIS, MN

Note to Librarians, Teachers, and Parents:

Blastoff! Readers are carefully developed by literacy experts and combine standards-based content with developmentally appropriate text.

Level 1 provides the most support through repetition of high-frequency words, light text, predictable sentence patterns, and strong visual support.

Level 2 offers early readers a bit more challenge through varied simple sentences, increased text load, and less repetition of high-frequency words.

Level 3 advances early-fluent readers toward fluency through increased text and concept load, less reliance on visuals, longer sentences, and more literary language.

Level 4 builds reading stamina by providing more text per page, increased use of punctuation, greater variation in sentence patterns, and increasingly challenging vocabulary.

Level 5 encourages children to move from "learning to read" to "reading to learn" by providing even more text, varied writing styles, and less familiar topics.

Whichever book is right for your reader, Blastoff! Readers are the perfect books to build confidence and encourage a love of reading that will last a lifetime!

This edition first published in 2020 by Bellwether Media, Inc.

Library of Congress Cataloging-in-Publication Data

Names: Rathburn, Betsy, author.
Title: Tsunamis / by Betsy Rathburn.
Description: Minneapolis, MN : Bellwether Media, Inc., [2020] | Series: Blastoff! Readers. Natural Disasters | Audience: Ages 5-8. | Audience: K to grade 3. | Includes bibliographical references and index.
Identifiers: LCCN 2019003808 (print) | LCCN 2019010222 (ebook) | ISBN 9781618915696 (ebook) | ISBN 9781644870280 (hardcover : alk. paper) | ISBN 9781618917492 (pbk. : alk. paper)
Subjects: LCSH: Tsunamis--Juvenile literature. | Natural disasters--Juvenile literature.
Classification: LCC GC221.5 (ebook) | LCC GC221.5 .R38 2020 (print) | DDC 551.46/37--dc23
LC record available at https://lccn.loc.gov/2019003808

Editor: Al Albertson Designer: Josh Brink

Printed in the United States of America, North Mankato, MN

Table of Contents

What Are Tsunamis?

Tsunamis are powerful ocean waves. They can cause a lot of **destruction**.

Most tsunamis form in the Pacific Ocean. They are common around the **Ring of Fire**.

How Do Tsunamis Form?

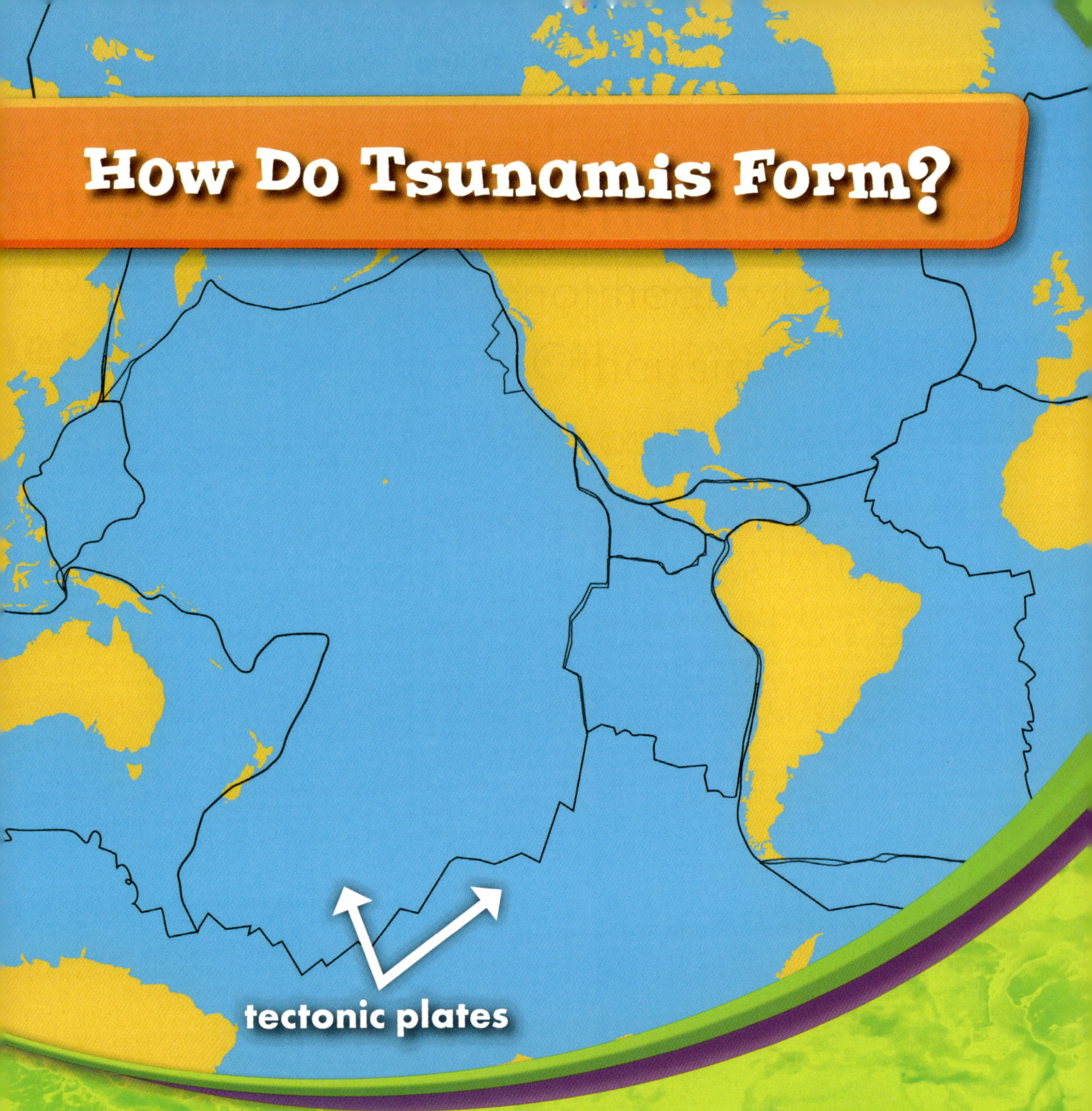

Most tsunamis are caused by earthquakes. The waves form when **tectonic plates** shift deep below Earth's surface.

Volcanic **eruptions** or underwater **landslides** can also lead to tsunamis. Even large **meteorite** strikes can cause tsunamis!

volcanic eruption

The energy from these events moves ocean water. Small, fast waves flow from the tsunami's **origin**.

Waves slow down as they get closer to shore. But they grow in energy. They build into huge walls of water!

How Tsunamis Form

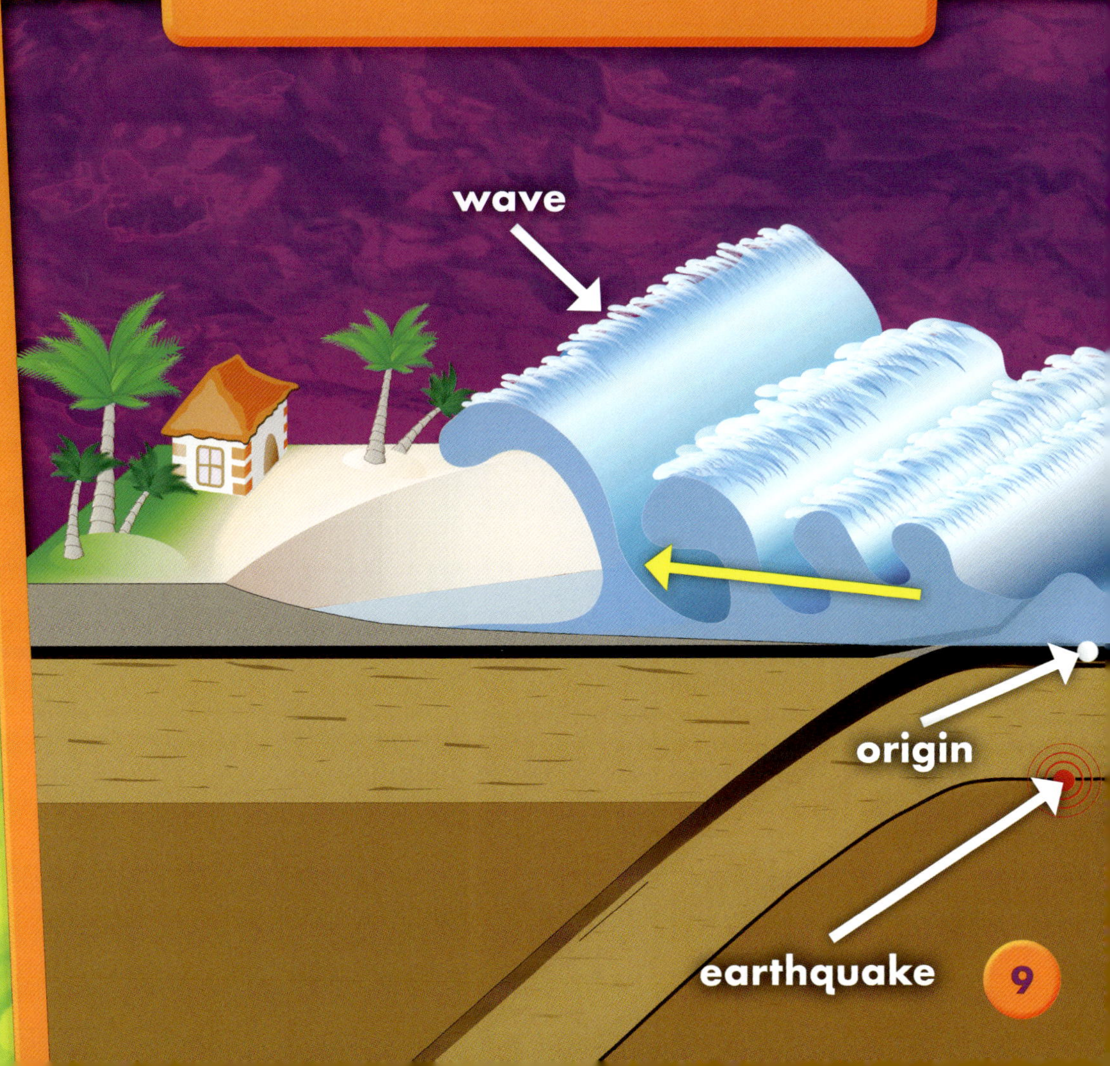

Tsunami Damage

Tsunamis cause a lot of damage to **coastal** areas. The waves damage buildings. They destroy roads and bridges.

Debris left by **receding** waves may block roads. People cannot get to school or work. Injured people cannot reach the hospital.

Power outages are common after tsunamis. There may be no electricity for days or weeks.

Tsunamis can also wash away oil and gas. These harmful materials can **pollute** drinking water.

polluted water

Some people may lose their jobs and homes. They stay in crowded shelters. It takes months or years to recover.

The **Tsunami Intensity Scale** measures tsunami damage. The biggest waves cause lasting problems!

tsunami shelter

Tsunami Intensity Scale

Levels 1 to 3: small wave

- seen or felt only by people in boats
- no damage

Levels 4 to 6: medium wave

- seen or felt by most on boats and on shore
- some small damage from flooding

Levels 7 to 9: large wave

- seen or felt by everyone in the area
- a lot of damage to vehicles and buildings

Levels 10 to 12: huge wave

- most people near coast washed away
- most or all buildings, vehicles, and roads damaged or destroyed

Predicting Disaster

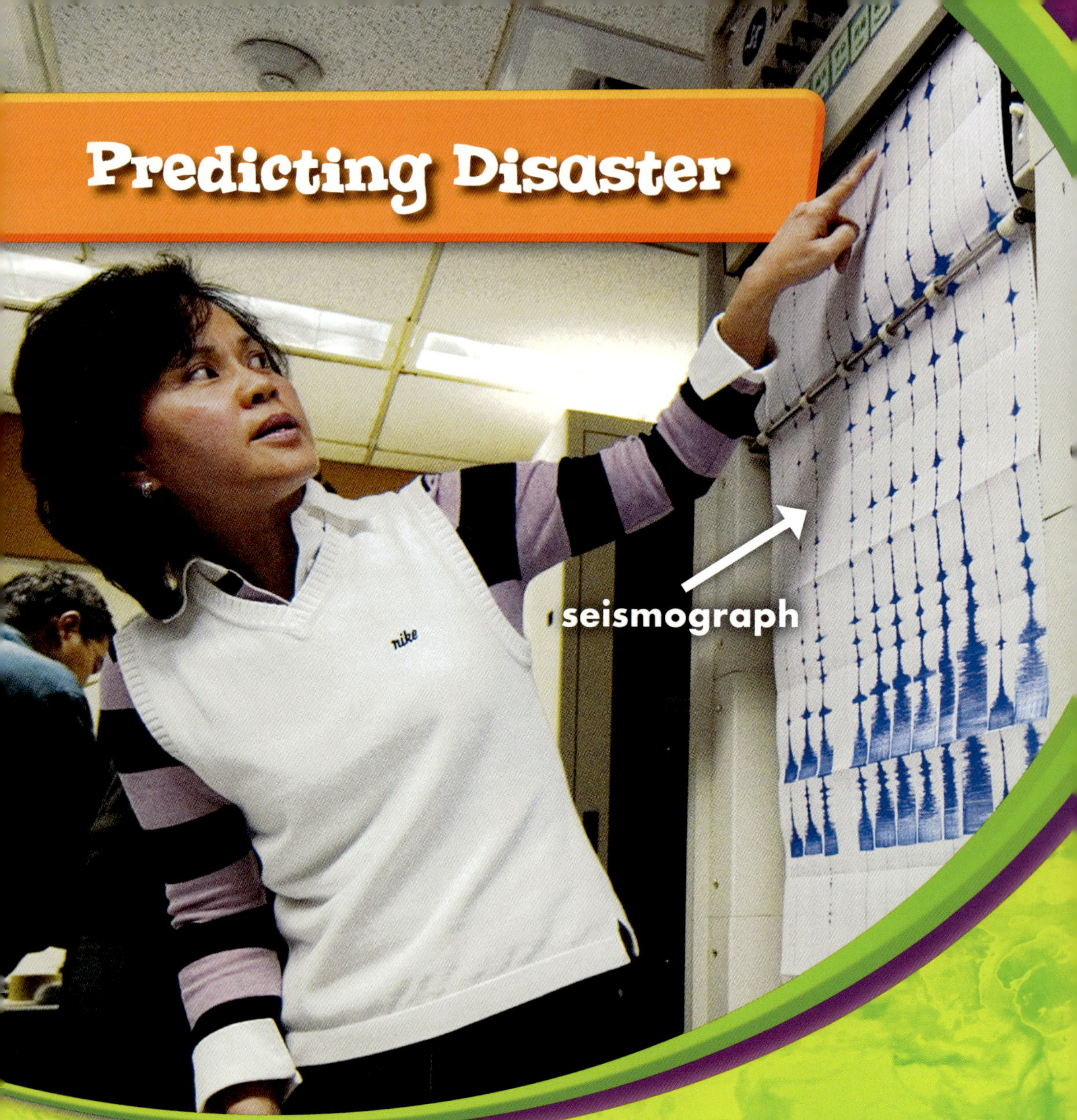

Scientists use **seismographs** to measure earthquakes. Large earthquakes may mean a tsunami is coming!

Special **buoys** measure the sea level. Rising water tells scientists the size and direction of tsunamis.

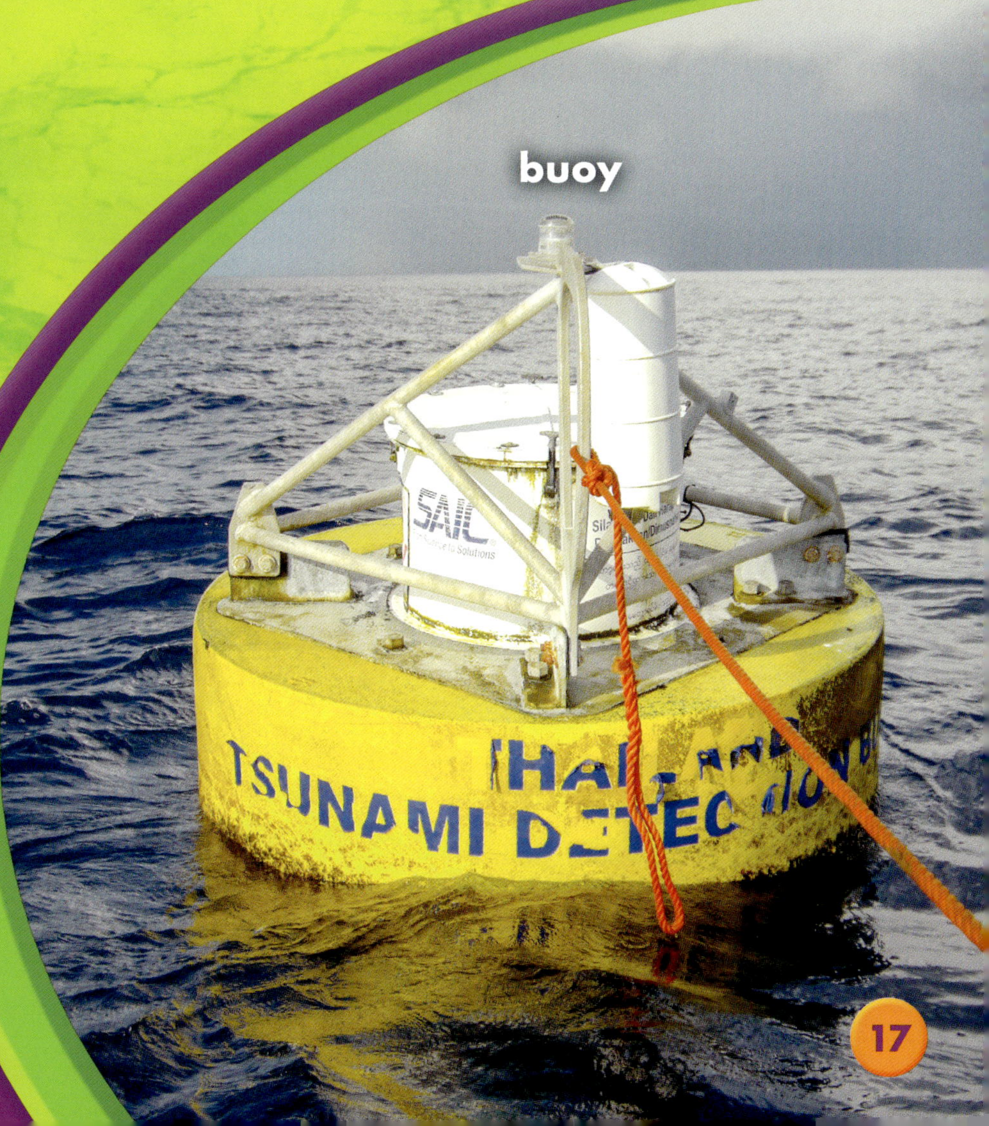

Experts may tell people to **evacuate**. But people may not hear warnings in time. Other signs can help keep people safe.

If water suddenly recedes, a tsunami could be near. A tall wall of water could also be a tsunami!

evacuation

Tsunami Profile

Name: Boxing Day tsunami

Date: December 26, 2004

Location: Indian Ocean countries such as Indonesia, Sri Lanka, India, Thailand, Bangladesh, and others

Damage to Property:
- 141,000 houses destroyed
- hundreds of schools destroyed
- nearly $10 billion in damage

Damage to People:
- almost 300,000 lives lost, mostly
- about 1.7 million people left without a home
- thousands of children lost parents

Boxing Day tsunami damage in Indonesia

Tsunamis affect low coastal areas. These powerful waves are difficult to escape. If one comes near, head to higher ground.

Tsunamis ruin entire cities. These natural disasters are harmful for everyone around!

Glossary

buoys–floating objects that mark a location in water

coastal–near the shore

debris–the remains of something destroyed

destruction–damage that cannot be repaired

eruptions–events in which volcanoes force out lava and ash

evacuate–to leave a unsafe area

landslides–events in which objects suddenly move down a slope

meteorite–space rocks that hit Earth

origin–the point where a tsunami begins

pollute–to make dirty or unusable

power outages–events in which no electricity is available

receding–moving or backing away

Ring of Fire–the area around the Pacific Ocean where most earthquakes occur; the Ring of Fire gets it name from the many volcanoes around its edges.

seismographs–tools used to measure the power of seismic waves

tectonic plates–the layers of Earth's crust that move

Tsunami Intensity Scale–a scale that measures the strength of tsunamis from 1 to 12

To Learn More

AT THE LIBRARY

Maurer, Tracy. *The World's Worst Tsunamis.* North Mankato, Minn.: Capstone Press, 2019.

McAneney, Caitie. *Slammed by Tsunamis.* New York, N.Y.: PowerKids Press, 2018.

Perish, Patrick. *Survive a Tsunami.* Minnetonka, Minn.: Bellwether Media, 2017.

ON THE WEB

FACTSURFER

Factsurfer.com gives you a safe, fun way to find more information.

1. Go to www.factsurfer.com.

2. Enter "tsunamis" into the search box and click 🔍.

3. Select your book cover to see a list of related web sites.

Index

The images in this book are reproduced through the courtesy of: Amanda Carden, cover (hero); Herwin Bahar, cover (houses); dharmakurniawan, cover (cars); ArchonCodex, cover (water); mTaira, CIP (house); Raul Mellado Ortiz, CIP (wave); JIJI PRESS/ Getty Images, p. 4; ghost design, p. 6; LukaKikina, p. 7; Dzmitry Melnikau, p. 8; Designua, p. 9; fiki j bhayangkara, p. 10; DEDDEDA/ Alamy, p. 11; Mark Pearson/ Alamy, p. 12; Archive Image/ Alamy, p. 13; Robert Gilhooly/ Alamy, p. 14; Grans Delian, p. 15; STR/ AP Images, p. 16; BNK Maritime Photographer, p. 17; ZUMA Press, Inc./ Alamy, p. 18; PJF Military Collection/ Alamy, p. 19; Frans Delian, p. 20; Kyodo News/ Getty Images, p. 21.